Diet recommendations during TCM - Lung - Phlegm-Heat in the Lungs

Please check these recommendations always with a nutrition consultant, therapist, doctor or dietician. The recipes and the list of ingredients are supporting the conventional medical therapy. The calorie disclosures of fresh ingredients (fruit and vegetables) vary according to quality and time of harvest. The contents were checked by a dietician and a nutrition consultant for the Traditional Chinese Medicine (TCM).

Author:
©2020 Josef Miligui
www.ebns.at

AF188846

Source:
The lists are created from the EBNS database for nutritional counseling. The database is used by dietitians, therapists and doctors for advising the patient / client.

Literature:
The specialist literature and the training documents of the German and Austrian dietary and traditional Chinese medicine serve as a knowledge base. We have used the documents as a basis of knowledge, adapted it to our experience and completed them.
http://nutribook.info/

Production and publishing:
BoD – Books on Demand, Norderstedt
ISBN: 9783750414037

(Book: E230)

Diet recommendations for TCM - Lung - Phlegm-Heat in the Lungs

1 Treatment strategy

Dissolve the mucus, cool the heat, lower the lungs, tone the spleen, calm the cough.
Avoid hot / warm - more refreshing foods.

2 Avoid

Poor nutritional style, cold drinks, no meat 4 hours before sleep, too much bread, cereals, too much raw food, cold foods / drinks, dairy products, tropical fruits, fruit juices, denatured food, factory sugar, fried, breaded and fat. See also: moist heat in the spleen.

3 Breakfast

	kkal. per serving
Adzuki Bean and Rice Soup	199
Cooling rice dish with grapefruit	234
Potato-basil soup	95
Radishjuice	9
Tea from ground	2
Tea from thyme	0
Tsampa	139

4 Snack

Adzuki Bean and Rice Soup	199

5 Lunch

Adzuki Bean and Rice Soup	199
Cooling rice dish with grapefruit	234
Potato-basil soup	95
Radishjuice	9
Tea from ground	2
Tea from thyme	0
Tsampa	139

6 Afternoon

7 Dinner

8 Any time

9 Recipes

(rec.) = You can use more.
(little) = You should use less than specified
(omit) = omit.

9.1 Adzuki Bean and Rice Soup

Reduces moisture, directs down, reduces gastrointestinal heat, builds up essence, strengthens muscles after
heat illness, builds up body fluids.
Cooking time approx. 2 hours
Calories p. portion: 199
1 portions

Quantity of ingredients
Adzuki beans 8 table spoons / 40g. (rec.) - neutral - sweet, sour .... water
Rice round grain 2 table spoons / 20g. (yes) - neutral - sweet .... metal
Water 1 1/2 cups / 200g. (yes) - cool - salty .... earth
Honey 1 table spoon / 8g. () - cold - sweet .... earth

Cooking instructions:
Boil soaked adzuki beans and round grain rice in a ratio of 4: 1 in water until a thin pulp has formed. Sweet as needed; possibly puree.

Effect: This recipe strengthens kidney, spleen and stomach and is particularly suitable for mothers with too little milk flow.

9.2 Basic recipe for a vegetable soup, nutritious

Strengthens spleen and lung, regulates Qi flow, builds up Qi, dries out, passes downwardly, strengthens
stomach Qi.
Cooking time approx. 2-3 hours
Calories p. portion: 48
5 portions
Allergens: L

Quantity of ingredients

Olive oil 1 table spoon / 4g. (yes) - cool - sweet.. earth
Onion white 1 piece / 60g. () - warm - acrid .... metal
Carrot 3 pieces / 200g. (yes) - neutral - sweet .... earth
Parsnip 3/8 lbs - 6oz / 150g. (yes) - cool - bitter.. fire
Celery root 1 cup / 100g. (yes) - cool - sweet.. earth
Ginger fresh 1/2 teaspoon / 2g. (rec.) - warm - acrid .... metal
Lemon 1/2 piece / 25g. () - cold - sour ....wood
Juniper berry 6 pieces / 6g. () - warm - sweet, acrid, bitter .... fire
Thyme dried 1 pinch / 1g. (yes) - warm - bitter... metal
Lovage 1 table spoon / 3g. () - warm - acrid, bitter.................................... metal
Bay leaf 2 leaves / 1g. (little) - warm - acrid ....*
Salt 1 pinch / 1g. (rec.) - cold - salty.. water
Water 3 cups / 650g. (yes) - cool - salty... earth

Cooking instructions:

Cut the vegetables into cubes.
Heat oil in hot pot, fry shortly onions and vegetables.
Add cold water, then add ginger, bay leaf and lemon juice.
Season with juniper, thyme and lovage. Cover for 2 - 3 hours on a low heat and simmer.
The used vegetables should be thrown away.
The basic recipe serves as a soup base and to refine vegetables, legumes or cereals.
If you want to eat vegetable soup immediately, add the desired vegetables half an hour before.
Refrigerate for later use.

9.3 Basmati rice + Zucchini tofu dish

Converts mucus, reduces heat, builds up Qi, nourishes fluids, harmonizes spleen and stomach, forces lung Qi.
Cooking time approx. 20 min
Calories p. portion: 146
4 portions
Allergens: E

Quantity of ingredients

Soy Tofu 5/8 lbs - 8oz / 250g. (yes) - cool - sweet .... earth
Olive oil 2 table spoons / 6g. (yes) - cool - sweet....................................... earth
Coriander 1/2 teaspoon / 4g. () - warm - acrid .... metal
Ginger fresh 1/2 teaspoon / 4g. (rec.) - warm - acrid .... metal
Rice Basmati 1/2 cup / 60g. (yes) - neutral - sweet.................................... metal
Water 3 cups / 200g. (yes) - cool - salty... earth
Zucchini 1 piece / 700g. (yes) - cool - sweet .... earth

Cooking instructions:
Cut tofu cubes and marinate with olive oil, tamari, crushed coriander and ginger. Leave at least 1 hour.

Cook Basmati rice with the water. You can season with onion and cardamom.
Roast zucchini and tofu in pan in the hot oil for approx. 5-7 min.
Serve rice and tofu on a plate.
Add the parsley.

Can also be used as a salad for the home and on the go.

9.4 Cooling rice dish with grapefruit

Lowers lung Qi, nourishes fluids, dissolves mucus, dries out, passes downwardly, warms the stomach and spleen, harmonizes the intestine, forces Qi, reduces moisture, strengthens Qi and Kidney Jing, moisturizes, relaxes, builds up Qi, spreads.
Cooking time approx. 20 min
Calories p. portion: 234
4 portions
Allergens: GHO

Quantity of ingredients
Rice round grain 1 cup / 120g. (yes) - neutral - sweet .... metal
Water 5 cups / 600g. (yes) - cool - salty .... earth
Hazelnuts 2 table spoons / 20g. () - neutral - sweet .... earth
Raisins 2 table spoons / 20g. () - warm - sweet .... earth
Agave nectar 1 table spoon / 10g. (yes) - cool - sweet ....*
Salt 1 pinch / 0,2g. (rec.) - cold - salty .... water
Almond puree 1 table spoon / 10g. () - neutral - sweet .... earth
Grapefruit (Pomelo) 1 piece / 200g. (rec.) - cool - sweet, sour .... fire
Butter organic 2 teaspoons / 20g. (yes) - neutral - sweet .... earth

Cooking instructions:
Preparation on the eve: Pour round grain rice into cold water and cook. Soak chopped hazelnuts and raisins in some hot water overnight.

In the morning: Stir in a little hot water some agave syrup; add the rice and heat; add a small pinch of salt, almond paste, chopped grapefruit, the soaked chopped hazelnuts and raisins and mix; Serve with a small piece of butter.

9.5 Potato-basil soup

Strengthens stomach Qi, moisturizes, relaxes, builds up Qi, spreads, forces Qi, forces spleen, relieves inflammation, spreads, strengthens spleen and liver, regulates Qi flow.
Cooking time approx. 25 min
Calories p. portion: 96
4 portions
Allergens: L

Quantity of ingredients

Water 2 cups / 450g. (yes) - cool - salty .... earth
Potato 4 pieces / 200g. (yes) - neutral - sweet .... earth
Carrot 2 pieces / 100g. (yes) - neutral - sweet .... earth
Celery root 1 piece / 500g. (yes) - cool - sweet .... earth
Pepper (ground) 1 pinch / 0,5g. () - warm - acrid .... metal
Ground 1 pinch / 1g. (rec.) - warm - acrid .... metal
Garlic 1 clove / 3g. () - hot - acrid .... metal
Salt 1 pinch / 1g. (rec.) - cold - salty .... water
Lemon 1 teaspoon / 3g. () - cold - sour .... wood
Basil (fresh) 1 Bunch / 50g. (rec.) - warm - acrid, bitter .... metal
Sugar cane sugar 1 pinch / 1g. () - cool - sweet .... earth
Olive oil 1 table spoon / 10g. (yes) - cool - sweet .... earth

Cooking instructions:

Peeled and chopped 4 medium potatoes in a pot of hot water and 2 chopped medium carrots, a piece of celery root, a pinch of pepper, a pinch of ground cumin, crushed a small clove of garlic, a pinch of salt, 1 teaspoon of lemon juice, simmer until the Vegetables is soft.

Add 1 bunch finely chopped basil into one half of the soup and puree everything; stir in the other half of the basil; with rose paprika, a pinch of whole cane sugar, 1 tablespoon of olive oil or butter, freshly ground pepper, salt to taste.

9.6 Radishjuice

Nourishes the lungs and spleen, distributes mucus, Dissolves mucus, dissolves stagnation, directs upwards.
Cooking time approx. 10 min
Calories p. portion: 9
1 portions

Quantity of ingredients
Radish (white, green) 1/2 piece / 50g. (yes) - cool - sweet, acrid .... metal
Water 1 cup / 120g. (yes) - cool - salty .... earth

Cooking instructions:
Make the radish juice with the juicer or buy it at the food store.
The fresh press juice is extracted from the root.
For healing purposes one prefers the black radish because of its sharpness.
The pungent taste is due to the mustard oils in the radish juice.
They stimulate bile-juice production in the liver. This has two different effects in our body. The appetite and
digestion are promoted and alleviates bile and liver disease.
Drink in small sips.

9.7 Smoothie celery carrot (BIRRS)

Nourishes juices, strengthens spleen and liver, regulates qi flow, relaxes, builds up qi. Moves liver-qi, reduces
cold-evil.
Cooking time approx. 10 Min.
Calories p. portion: 111
2 portions
Allergens: L

Quantity of ingredients
Carrot 5/8 oz / 200g. (yes) - neutral - sweet .... earth
Celery sticks 10 cups / 100g. (yes) - cool - sweet .... earth
Apple (sweet) 5/8 oz / 200g. (rec.) - cool - sweet, sour .... earth
Basil (fresh) 2 table spoons / 5g. (rec.) - warm - acrid, bitter .... metal
Ginger fresh 1/8 oz / 5g. (rec.) - warm - acrid .... metal
Reishi mushroom 1 pinch / 1g. (rec.) - cool - sweet .... earth
Salt 1 pinch / 1g. (rec.) - cold - salty .... water

Cooking instructions:
Wash and clean vegetables and divide into pieces. Puree all ingredients in a blender.

9.8 Tea from chamomile

Reduces internal wind and heat, cools liver.
Cooking time approx. 10 min
Calories p. portion: 0
1 portions

Quantity of ingredients
Chamomile 1 teaspoon / 3g. (rec.) - cool - sweet, bitter.................................... *
Water 1 cup / 120g. (yes) - cool - salty.. earth

Cooking instructions:
Heat the water till it boils and put it aside. Chamomile flowers added and 10 min. to let go.

9.9 Tea from ground

Reduces mucus and moist heat in the liver and gallbladder, against liver Qi stagnation, spleen qi deficiency, spleen and kidney Yang- deficiency.
Cooking time approx. 10 min
Calories p. portion: 2
4 portions

Quantity of ingredients
Ground 1 teaspoon / 3g. (rec.) - warm - acrid .... metal
Water 2 cup / 500g. (yes) - cool - salty.. earth

Cooking instructions:
Heat the water till it boils and put it aside. Add crushed cumin and leave for 10 min. to let go. Sweet to taste with honey. Strain when pouring.

Drink 1 cup 2 times a day.

9.10 Tea from thyme

Converts mucus, forces lungs and spleen, dries out, passes downwardly.
Cooking time approx. 10 min
Calories p. portion: 0
4 portions

Quantity of ingredients
Thyme 3 table spoons / 6g. (rec.) - warm - bitter ....*
Water 2 cup water / 500g. (yes) - cool - salty..earth

Cooking instructions:
Heat the water till it boils and put it aside. Add thyme and 10 min. to let go. Strain. Sweet to taste with honey.
Drink 2 to 3 cups daily by mouth

9.11 Tsampa

Reduces internal heat, dissolves mucus, detoxifies.
Cooking time approx. 5 min
Calories p. portion: 140
2 portions
Allergens: A

Quantity of ingredients
Tsampa (roasted) 4 table spoons / 30g. (yes) - cold - sweet, little salty .... earth
Green tea 1 cup / 120g. (yes) - cool - sweet, bitter .... fire
Water 1 cup / 120g. (yes) - cool - salty.. earth

Cooking instructions:
Tsampa is traditionally made with tea.
The tsampa is poured into a bowl and doused with tea, part of which is drunk and the remainder made into a dough-like mass with tsampa. You can also pour the tea first; In any case, it takes some skill to achieve the right balance of tsampa and liquid. The two substances are usually mixed with your fingers. It is recommended to add yak butter to improve taste and stability.

10 Effects of food

10.1 Use ingredients: recommendable

Adzuki beans
Apple (sour)
Apple (sweet)
Apple puree
Basil
Basil (fresh)
Bitter orange peel
Black caraway
Blackberry leaves
Boletus mushroom
Chamomile
Champignon
Chenpi (chinese tangerine bowl)
Coix (seeds) YiYi Ren
Fresh cheese from soya
Ginger fresh
Grapefruit (Pomelo)
Grapefruit juice
Ground
Kombu seaweed (Saccharina japonica)
Kumquats
Lemon Balm (fresh)
Lotus roots
Marjoram
Miso
Miso black (fermented)
Nasturtium (nose-twister or nose-tweaker)
Nettles
Nori, purple seaweed, red algae
Orange dried peel
Orange grated peel
Orange peel
Oregano dried
Oregano fresh
Pork skin
Reishi mushroom
Salt
Salt (herbal)
Sugar substitute (sweetener)
Thyme
Yam root, yam root tuber

10.2 Use ingredients: yes

Agave nectar
Angelica root
Apple juice (natural cloudy)
Apricots
Apricots juice
Banchatee (green tea)
Barley
Barley flour
Barley not peeled
Basic recipe for a fish soup
Basic recipe for a vegetable soup (nutritious)
Black fungus mushroom
Boxhorn clover seeds
Bread roll
Breadcrumbs (wheat bread, bread roll)
Butter (half fat)
Butter organic
Carob flour, St. john's bread
Carrot
Carrot (Early Carrot)
Carrot juice without sugar
Celery root
Celery sticks
Chinese cabbage
Cranberries
Fennel
Fructose (glucose)
Ginger powder
Green tea
Hijiki
Lotus seeds
Millet
Millet flakes
Mu Erh Mushroom
Multi-grain bread (gray bread)
Olive oil
Parsley root
Parsnip
Pearl barley
Pearl barley
Peas, green
Potato
Potato (mealy)
Potato flour
Psyllium seed
Radish (white, green, purple-red)
Radish black
Raspberry leaf tea
Red beet

Rice (fragrance)
Rice (Gaoliang / Sorghum)
Rice (whole grain)
Rice Basmati
Rice long grain rice
Rice mash
Rice red
Rice round grain
Rice sticky
Rice sweet
Savory
Soy Tofu
Soy Tofu smoked
Stevia (candyleaf, sweetleaf)
Thyme dried
Tsampa (roasted barley flour)
Turnip
Turnips
Water
Wormwood herb
Yarrow
Zucchini

10.3 Use ingredients: little

Avocado
Barley malt
Bay leaf
Beef fillet
Beef lungs (calf)
Beef meat
Beef meat (calf)
Beef Oxtail pieces
Beef soup meat
Black beans
Brazil nuts
Broad beans (thick beans)
Broccoli
Brussels sprouts
Bush beans
Butter beans white
Camembert
Cauliflower
Chocolate
Chocolate (Diabetic)
Clarified butter
Clementine
Cream (30% fat)
Cream sour 10%
Cream sour 20%
Cream, sweet 30%
Currants (black)
Currants (red)
Duck (slaughtered)
Dyer's broom herb
Edam cheese
Emmental cheese
Feta cheese
Fish innards
Fish sauce
Fox nut, gorgon nut, makhana
French beans
Fresh cheese with herbs
Gail plum
Gelatin white
Grape juice red
Grape juice white
Hokkaido pumpkin
Horehound leaves
Kidney beans (red)
Kohlrabi
Kudzu
Lamb's lettuce
Lima beans
Linseed
Linseed (crushed)
Mascarpone cheese
Mayonnaise 50%
Medlar
Mung bean
Mung bean sprouting
Mustard Dijon
Nectarine
Noodles (wheat) with egg
Noodles (wheat, lasagne) with egg
Noodles (wheat, ribbon noodles) with egg
Noodles (wheat, spaghetti) with egg
Noodles (whole grain) with egg
Oyster mushroom
Passion fruit
Pepper powder (hot)
Peppers powder
Pinto beans speckled
Pork brain
Pork ham
Pork ham cooked
Pork meat
Processed cheese 12%
Puff pastry
Radish
Red cabbage
Rice black
Rice starch
Rice variety any

Rice wild (nature rice)
Rose blossom tea
Savoy cabbage / kale
Sheep's milk yoghurt
Soy flour
Soy noodles
Soybeans
Soybeans, black
Soybeans, yellow
Spurdog (spiny dogfish, Schillerlocken)
Turkey breast meat
Turkey ham
Turmeric (yellow root)
Wax gourd
Wheat
Wheat bulgur
Wheat flatbread/pita bread
Wheat flour
Wheat flour whole grain
Wheat germ oil
Wheat semolina
Wheat semolina for children
White beans
White bread (baguette)
White bread (wheat bread)
White breadcrumbs
White cabbage
White dumpling bread (wheat bread cut into chunks)
Whole grain bread
Wholemeal flour

10.4 Do not use contra-acting foods

Agar agar (kelp)
Almond
Almond marzipan
Almond milk
Almond puree
Aloe juice
Amaranth
Amaranth Pops
Anchovy / Sardine
Anise (Common Fennel)
Apricot
Apricot dried
Apricot jam
Apricot nectar
Arrowroot
Artichoke
Asparagus (green or white)
Aubergine
Balm
Bamboo shoots
Banana
Banana (cooking banana)
Basic recipe for a beef soup
Basic recipe for a beef soup (warming)
Basic recipe for a chicken soup (warming)
Basic recipe for a duck soup
Basic recipe for a rice soup (Congee)
Batavia
Bean oil
Beans (green, fresh)
Beef bone marrow
Beef heart
Beef kidney
Beef liver
Beef meatbones
Beef stomach
Beer (alcohol-free)
Beer (Pils)
Beer (Top-fermented German dark beer)
Berry juice
Bitter Herb liqueur
Bitter melon
Black tea
Blackberry dried (unripe fruit)
Blackberry jam
Blackberry´s
Black-eyed peas
Blueberry
Blueberry dried
Blueberry jam
Blueberry juice
Bocksdorn fruits (Fructus Lycii, Goji, goji berry
Borage
Borage oil
Brown ale
Buckwheat
Buckwheat (roasted) Kasha
Buckwheat whole grain
Bulgur (cereals)
Burdock root tea
Buttermilk
Calamari
Cantaloupe
Capers in olive oil
Carambola (Star fruit)
Cardamom
Carp

Cashews
Caviar
Cereal coffee
Channa-Dal
Chanterelle
Chard
Cherry
Cherry (sour)
Cherry compote
Cherry juice
Chervil
Chervil dried
Chestnuts
Chicken egg
Chicken heart
Chicken liver
Chicken meat
Chicken stomach
Chicken yolk
Chickpeas
Chickweed
Chicory
Chili (pod or ground)
Chives
Chlorella (fresh water)
Chrysanthemum blossom tea
Cinnamon ground
Cinnamon sticks
Clementines
Clove
Cocoa
Coconut fat
Coconut flakes
Coconut grated
Coconut meat
Coconut milk
Cod
Codfish
Coffee
Cooking oil
Coriander
Coriander (fresh)
Corn
Corn (roasted)
Corn Grease (Polenta)
Corn silk tea
Couscous
Cow's milk (1.5% fat)
Cow's milk (whole milk 3.5% fat)
Crab
Cranberry
Cranberry
Cranberry jam
Cranberry juice
Créme fraiche cheese
Cress
Crucian
Cucumber
Cucumber (spicy cucumber)
Cumin (Caraway seed)
Curcuma
Curd cheese 20%
Curd cheese 40%
Currant (black)
Currant (red)
Currant (white)
Curry
Curry paste red
Daisy
Dandelion (young plants)
Dandelion juice
Dandelionroots tea
Dates dried
Dates red
Deer meat
Deer meat
Dill
Duck (heart)
Dulse (seaweed)
Eel
Eel smoked
Elderberries
Elderberry blossom tee
Endive salad
Evening primrose oil
Fennel seeds ground
Fennel tea
Feta cheese
Fig
Fig dried
Fish pieces mixed (fresh water)
Fish remains
Flower pollen
Fresh cheese
Freshwater fish
Fruit tea
Galangal
Garlic
Gelee Royal
Gentian root
Ginger oil
Ginkgo fruit
Ginseng root
Goat
Goat and sheep's milk
Goat cheese
Goose
Goose egg

Goose parts
Gooseberry
Gorgonzola
Gouda cheese
Gourd
Grapefruit dried peel
Grapes red
Grapes white
Grass carp
Green spelt
Ground caraway
Halibut (Flatfish)
Hawthorn
Hazelnuts
Herbs bitter
Herbs of Provence
Herbs various
Herbs wild
Herring
Hibiscus
Honey
Hyssop
Iceberg lettuce
Jasmine blossoms tee
Juniper berry
Kaki plum
Kefir
Kiwi
Kukicha tea
Lamb bones
Lamb kidneys
Lamb liver
Lamb meat
Lamb shoulder
Lamb's lettuce
Leaf salads (bitter)
Leek
Lemon
Lemon juice
Lemon peel
Lemongrass
Lentils
Lentils black
Lentils red
Lentils yellow
Lettuce
Licorice root tea
Lime
Lime blossom tea
Linseed oil
Lobster
Longane
Lovage
Lychee
Lychee in Preserved
Mackerel
Mallow (Malva sylvestris) blossom tea
Malt
Mango
Mango juice
Manioc flour
Maple syrup
Margarine
Margarine (diet)
Mediterranean fish (cod, plaice,
haddock, sea
Mineral water
Mirabelle plum
Miso paste (soy bean paste)
Mold cheese
Morel (black, dried)
Morel, dried
Mozzarella
Mulberry fruit
Mulled Wine Spice
Mullet
Mussels
Mustard
Mustard seeds
Mustard sweet
Mutton
Mutton
Nutmeg
Oat
Oat flakes (whole grain)
Oat flakes roasted
Oat flour
Oat fusion (baby food)
Oat meal
Oat milk
Octopus
Okra
Olives
Onion (shallot)
Onion (spring onion)
Onion read
Onion white
Orange
Orange blossom
Orange jam
Orange juice
Oyster shell powder
Oysters
Papaya
Parmesan
Parsley
Passion blossoms tea
Peaches

Peaches (canned)
Peanut (roasted)
Peanut butter
Peanut oil
Peanuts
Pear
Pear juice
Peas
Pepper Cayenne
Pepper white (ground)
Peppercorns
Peppermint
Pepperoni, red, pitted, halved
Peppers
Peppers (rose peppers)
Peppers (sweet)
Perch
Pheasant
Pickle
Pigeon
Pimento
Pine nuts
Pineapple
Pineapple (from a can)
Pineapple juice without sugar
Pistachios
Plaice
Plum
Plum dried
Plums
Pomegranate
Poppy
Pork Bacon
Pork fat (lard)
Pork ham smoked
Pork heart
Pork knuckle
Pork Lard
Pork liver
Pork sausage (Bratwurst)
Pork stomach
processed cheese 30%
Pumpkin
Pumpkin seed oil
Pumpkin seeds
Quail
Quail egg
Quince
Quinoa
Rabbit
Rabbit liver
Rabbit meat
Radicchio
Radish horseradish
Radish leaves
Raisins
Rapeseed oil
Raspberry
Raspberry dried (immature)
Raspberry jam
Red berry (without sugar)
Red wine
Rhubarb
Rice flour
Rice malt
Rice noodles
Romaine lettuce / lettuce salad
Rose hip
Rose hip tea
Rose leaf tea
Rosefish
Rosemary
Rye
Rye flour
Rye wholemeal bread
Safflower (Dyer's thistle / Hong Hua)
Saffron
Sage
Sago (cereals)
Sake
Salmon
Salsify
Sauerkraut (cutted cabbage fermented)
Sea buckthorn
Seacrab
Sesame oil
Sesame oil roasted
Sesame paste (Tahini)
Sesame, black
Sesame, white
Shark
Sheep's milk
Sherry (whine)
Shiitake, dried
Shrimp
Shrimps
Sorrel
Sour cherries
Sour cream 15% fat
Sour milk
Sour milk cheese 20%
Sourdough
Soy sauce
Soya Cuisine (soy cream)
Soybean milk
Soybean oil
Soybeans, blacks, fermented
Spelled (Dark) bread

Spelled flakes
Spelled grain
Spelled semolina
Spelled wholemeal flour
Spinach
Spiny lobsters
Spirit
Star anise
Strawberries
Strawberry jam
Strawberry Juice
Sugar brown
Sugar candy white
Sugar cane sugar
Sugar fructose - fruit sugar
Sugar glucose - grapes sugar
Sugar Milk Sugar
Sugar molasses
Sugar white
Sunflower oil
Sunflower seeds
Sweet potato
Tabasco
Tangerine
Tarragon (Estragon)
Thistle oil
Tomato
Tomato dried
Trout
Tuna
Umeboshi paste
Umeboshi plums (Japanese apricots)
Valerian
Vanilla
Vanilla pod
Vanilla powder
Vanilla sugar natural
Vegetable juice
Vinegar (Apple vinegar)
Vinegar (Red wine vinegar)
Vinegar Aceto Balsamico
Vinegar Aceto Balsamico white
Wakame
Walnut oil
Walnuts
Walnuts roasted
Water hot
Watermelon
Wheat beer
Wheat bran
Wheat flakes
Wheatgrass juice
Whey
White wine
Wild boar meat
Wild garlic (garlic spinach)
Wild strawberries
Wormwood
Yarrow tea
Yeast
Yogi tea
Yogurt (natural, 1.5% fat)
Yogurt (natural, 3.5% fat)

11 Complementary

11.1 Coneflowers

Echinacea purpurea
preparation: Decoction
Activates Wie-Qi, strengthens lung- and stomach-Qi.
Use: finished preparations
The well-known complementary doctor Dr. med. However, Keith Block attributed Essiac only a weak antitumor effect and suggested that the healing results of the tea around the turn of the century may have been a lot better because of the significantly lower levels of stress on people with carcinogenic substances.

11.2 Eucalyptus

Eucalyptus globulus
preparation: Decoction
Eliminates heat-phlegm of the lungs, dissipates moisture-heat and wind-heat, strengthens Wei Qi.
9-15 g
Use: tea, essential oil
Not for children under the age of 12 or in the first trimester of pregnancy.

11.3 Horehound (common horehound)

Marrubium vulgare, herb.
preparation: Healing tea (infusion)
Dissects lung-mucus, draining, dries moisture, clears heat, toning Qi of middle, regulating Qi.
Pour 2 teaspoons of the tea into 250 ml of boiling water and leave for 10 minutes. Then sieve. Drink 2 to 3 cups per day as needed.
On the outside you can use the tea or dilute tincture in the form of envelopes, baths or washes. With this type of application one can relieve eczema.
Horehound also uses externally against ulcers and other wounds that do not want to heal.
Do not use during pregnancy, lactation or from people with heart disease.

11.4 Johnny Jump up

Viola tricolor
preparation: Healing tea (infusion)
Opening surface, dissipating wind-heat. Dissolves mucus heat.
It has been known since ancient times as a blood cleanser and uses it as a tea or compress for skin conditions, such as blemished complexion, acne or eczema. It also works diuretic and expectorant in cough.

11.5 Plantain

Plantago lanceolata/major, herb.
preparation: Healing tea (infusion)
Clears lung heat and dissipates heat-phlegm.
Plantain is one of the best herbs to break up the mucous deposits of the intestine. And he is one of the best blood cleaners.
Plantain is a good liverwort and also improves the function of the kidneys. It helps prevent bloating and diarrhea. Overall, he is one of the largest medicinal herbs of nature. It tastes delicious in a salad (along with dandelion leaves) and probably grows in your own backyard.

11.6 Reishi

Ganoderma lucidum
preparation: Different effects
Calms and nourishes the heart. Tonifies Qi and Xue, nourishes the blood. Induces heat and mucus.
Astringent.
As an addition to tea, cocoa or coffee. As capsules, extract, powder or whole mushroom.

11.7 Thujas or cedars leaves

Cacumen Biotae
preparation: Different effects
Cools blood. Clears heat and toxins. Induces mucus-heat. Moves blood. Regulates uterus.
10-15 g
For bleeding use external application.

11.8 Turmeric

Curcuma longa
preparation: Cooking addition
Eliminates moisture-heat, dissipates mucus-heat from the lungs. Eliminates heat from the stomach and intestines. Moves qi and blood. Active ingredients: eth. Oil, bitter substances, curcumin, starch

Turmeric or Tumeric - Has achieved impressive success in the treatment of carcinogens and mutagens in laboratory animals. Concentrated turmeric showed an increase in the glutathione S-transferase enzymes, which are essential for life and liver detoxification.

Medical applications: Amenorrhoea, anemia, arthritis, asthma, blood clots, cancer, candida, catarrh, anabolic, cough, dysentery, dysmenorrhea, eczema, winds, gallbladder disease, gallstones, gastritis, heart disease, hepatitis, high cholesterol, indigestion, irritable Intestines, jaundice, liver detoxification, liver protection, nausea, obesity, cerebral catarrh, skin diseases, including parasitic skin infections, traumas, urinary tract diseases, tumors of the uterus.

Properties: Alterative, analgesic, antibiotic, anti-coagulant (inhibits blood clotting) antifungal, anti-inflammatory, antioxidant, antiseptic, aromatic, astringent, cholagogue, circulation stimulating, digestive, the entry of the menstrual period promoting agent, liver-strengthening, stimulant, supports wound healing.
When blockade bile ducts or gallstones should be dispensed turmeric.

12 Basics of Nutrition

The basic principles of nutrition described herein are general recommendations. They are not aimed at a specific form of therapy. Recommendations concerning a therapy have priority.

12.1 Nutrition

Regular meals in a relaxed atmosphere. A warm breakfast is considered a good start into the day.
The main meals ought to be taken for lunch – supper in the early evening. Pay attention to feeling hungry or sated: don't eat too much nor remain hungry is the rule
Prepare the meals freshly from natural, regional products. Frozen, heat-conserved, industrially prepared or foodstuffs cooked in the microwave oven are rejected.
Choice of foodstuffs according to the season: more cooling food in summer, more warming food in winter.
Eat cooked food at least twice a day. Food and drinks ought to be lukewarm, never ice-cold or hot.
Raw vegetables, briefly cooked vegetables, freshly squeezed juices and mineral water are not recommended. Milk and dairy products are only included in the diet if they don't cause problems. Don't use therapeutic recipes over a longer period without consulting your doctor or therapist.

Varied food
Enjoy the diversity of foodstuffs. Characteristics of a balanced nutrition are variety, suitable combination and a balanced quantity of rich and low energy foodstuffs (on one hand avoiding undersupply with essential nutrients and on the other hand to take to many undesirable substances).

A lot of Cereal Products - and Potatoes
Bread, pasta, rice, cereal flakes (best wholemeal) as well as potatoes contain almost no fat, but many vitamins, mineral nutrients, trace elements, roughage and secondary plant substances. These foodstuffs ought to be taken with low-fat side dishes.

Vegetables and Fruit – „Take Five" every day ... 5 portions of vegetables and fruit a day, as fresh as possible, briefly cooked, or maybe one portion as a juice – ideal as a side dish to every meal as well as snack between meals: Thus a lot of vitamins, mineral nutrients as well as roughage and secondary plant substances

Daily milk and dairy products

Milk and Dairy Products every Day, once or twice per Week Fish; meat, sausages as well as eggs moderately. These foodstuffs contain valuable nutrients like calcium in the milk, iodine selenium and omega-3 fat acids in saltwater fish. Meat is favorable due to its high content of disposable iron and the vitamins B1, B6 and B12. Quantities of 300 – 600 g meat and sausage per week are sufficient. Prefer low-fat products, especially in meat- and dairy products.

Low-fat and fatty Foodstuffs

Fat supplies us with essential fat acids and fatty foodstuffs contain also fat-soluble vitamins. Fat is high in energy; therefore much fat in the food may cause overweight, possibly also cancer. Too many saturated fat acids may further a tendency for cardio-vascular diseases in the long term. Prefer vegetable oils and fats (e.g. rapeseed-, olive-, soya-oils and solid fats produced therefrom). Beware of invisible fat in meat- and dairy products, pastry and sweets as well as in fast-food and convenience foods. 70 – 90 g fat per day is sufficient.

Moderately Sugar and Salt

Take sugar and foods/drinks containing various kinds of sugar (e.g. glucose syrup) only occasionally. Use herbs and spices as well as a little salt creatively. Prefer salt containing iodine.

Plenty of Liquids

Water is absolutely essential. Drink 1-2 l liquids every day. Prefer water (with or without gas) and other low-calorie drinks. Alcoholic drinks should not be taken.

Tasty Dishes, carefully cooked

Cook the meals with as low temperatures and as short as possible, using little water and fat – this preserves the original taste, keeps the nutrients intact and prevents the production of harmful compounds.

Take time and enjoy the food

Take your Time and enjoy your Food
Eating consciously helps to eat right. The eye enjoys food, too. It's fun, invites to enjoy varied dishes and stimulates the feeling of satiety.

Watch your Weight and stay in Motion

A balanced diet and a lot of exercise and sport (30 – 60 min/day) are a healthy combination. The right weight furthers well-being and health.

Thermals, directional effectiveness, digestive power
There are various criteria for judging the effectiveness of herbs and foodstuffs.
The use of certain herbs and ingredients is based on observations of the effects on the body which these foodstuffs, herbs and spices show after having eaten them. The medical science has developed following system: Every ingredient or herb has a directional effectiveness. Furthermore, there are herbs which have a special effect on certain organs.
The basic condition for a healthy metabolism is to obtain sufficient energy from food and that the digestive process doesn't use too much energy. An easily digestible meal makes content and sated, doesn't cause flatulence and fatigue after the meal. The perfect spices increase the healthiness of our meals. Very often, just small doses of herbs and spices will suffice. They are not used to make us sated, but to help our digestive organs to digest the food.

12.2 Recipes

The recipes list the ingredients to be used and the cooking instructions show how the dish is prepared. The list of ingredients shows the concerned quantities as well as the relevance for the therapy. If you find „omit", try to comply or find an alternative from the „list of recommended foodstuffs". Mostly it shall result just in a small change of taste when you simply avoid this ingredient.
Mild cooking methods: boiling, stewing, poaching, steaming
Strong cooking methods: barbecuing, roasting, frying, smoking
Balanced cooking methods: deep-frying, baking brick
Deep-freezing and warming in the microwave oven should be avoided (denaturalization).

12.3 Foodstuffs

Foodstuffs have an effect on body and soul like medicinal herbs, only a very much milder one. Dietary advice is mainly based on regional foodstuffs. The knowledge about the effects of each foodstuff and the knowledge, when which foodstuff shall be used, is based on the school medicine. Use ecologic-organic products, if possible. As everything should be cooked for a long time due to a better digestability and very rarely eaten raw, the food agrees with everyone.
The classification of the foodstuffs according to their effect on the body is the basis in order to achieve a harmonious status of health.
Dietary advisors do not recommend certain foodstuffs for everyone. The individual diet is tailor-made for the individual constitution.

Buy only fresh and ripe fruit and vegetables. You ought to leave unripe fruit and vegetables and such with brown spots and wilted leaves behind in the market. In this case take deep-frozen goods (never ready-to-serve dishes!). Fruit and vegetables are deep-frozen immediately after harvesting and often contain more vitamins and minerals than the goods from the vegetable shelf. Whereas conserved or tinned goods contain very much less biological substances. Also, salt, sugar and others are mostly added to the latter. Never leave the foodstuffs in the water after washing them to avoid that many vital substances get drowned. Clean salads, fruit and vegetables immediately before serving.

Please make sure of the hygienic processing of foodstuffs. Clean your salads, fruit and vegetables carefully. When cooking with meat, prepare all ingredients first and then process the meat products. Clean the worktop and tools very carefully. Wooden surfaces ought to be treated with a mild disinfectant regularly in order to reduce germination.
Store fruit and vegetables separately, if possible. Harvested fruit and vegetables are still alive and emit e.g. ethylene gas, which makes other products ripen and age faster. Keep meat and fish in the closed packaging or store them in the fridge in closed containers.

12.4 Herbs

There are some basic rules for storing medicinal herbs. On principle, herbs must be protected from direct sunlight, humidity and heat.

Containers for the storage of herbs may be glasses, ceramic jars and even plastic containers. However, plastic is a rather unsuitable material and should only be a short-term solution. In case of glass containers, use a dark material.

Medicinal herbs cannot be kept for any long period. The shelf life of herbs is limited. However, it can be prolonged with suitable storage. The place should be dark, rather cool and absolutely dry. A wooden medicine cabinet, placed not directly next to a source of heat, would be ideal. Never buy large quantities of herbs so as not to have to throw them away. Label the container with the name of the herb and the date of harvesting or processing.

13 Other dietic-books

The following syndromes of dietetics, TCM or for a therapy supplement for cancer are available.

Dietetics

E001. Nutrition of the infant - baby food
E002. Nutrition during lactation
E003. Nutrition in old age
E004. Nutrition of children and adolescents
E005. Nutrition of athletes
E006. Light weight
E007. Pregnancy
E008. Full food

Protein and electrolyte - kidneys
E009. (hemodialysis) dialysis treatment
E010. Acute renal failure
E011. Chronic renal insufficiency
E012. Nephrotic syndrome
E013. Kidney stones (nephrolithiasis)

Gastrointestinal tract - pancreas
E014. Acute pancreatitis (inflammation of the pancreas)
E015. Chronic pancreatitis (inflammation of the pancreas)

Gastrointestinal tract - small intestine and large intestine
E016. Acute obstipation (constipation)
E017. Chronic obstipation (constipation)
E018. Colon irritabile
E019. Diverticulitis
E020. Acquired lactose intolerance (lactose malabsorption)
E021. Fructose malabsorption
E022. Glutensensitive enteropathy (celiac disease)
E023. Colectomy
E024. Short Bowel Syndrome

Gastrointestinal tract - liver, gallbladder, bile ducts
E025. Acute and chronic hepatitis (inflammation of the liver)
E026. Cholelithiasis (bile stones)
E027. fatty liver
E028. cirrhosis

Gastrointestinal tract - Stomach and duodenal intestine
E029. Acute gastritis
E030. Chronic gastritis
E031. Stomach bleeding
E032. Ulcus ventriculi and duodenal ulcer
E033. Condition after gastric surgery

Gastrointestinal tract - oral cavity and esophagus
E034. Stomatitis
E035. Esophageal carcinoma (esophageal cancer)
E036. Refluosophagitis (heartburn)

Special diseases
E037. Phenylketonuria (PKU)
E038. Rheumatic joint diseases

Metabolism
E039. Obesity (overweight)
E040. Diabetes mellitus
E041. Eating disorders (underweight)

Fat metabolism
E042. Hypercholesterolaemia (increased cholesterol level)
E043. Hepatic Encephalopathy

Heart and circulation
E044. Arteriosclerosis (arterial calcification)
E045. Heart insufficiency
E046. Hypertension
E047. Hyperuricaemia and gout

Changed nutrient requirements
E048. In case of fever
E049. For malignant diseases
E050. After burns
E051. Radiation and chemotherapy

CANCER
E100. Pancreatic cancer
E101. Bladder cancer
E102. Blood cancer (leukemia)
E103. Breast cancer
E104. Colorectal cancer
E105. Gastric cancer
E106. Kidney cancer
E107. Esophageal cancer

TCM
E200. Bladder - moisture heat in the bladder
E201. Bladder - moisture and cold in the bladder
E202. Bladder - emptiness and cold in the bladder
E203. Large intestine - external cold affects the large intestine
E204. Large intestine - moisture heat in the large intestine
E205. Large intestine - heat blocks the intestine II acute
E206. Large intestine - dryness of the colon
E207. Large intestine - Yang deficiency (cold)
E208. Heart - Blood insufficiency
E209. Heart - Blood stagnation
E210. Heart - Fire
E211. Heart - Hot mucus clogs the heart pores

E212. Heart - Cold mucus clogs the heart pores
E213. Heart - Qi deficiency
E214. Heart - Yang deficiency
E215. Heart - Yin deficiency
E216. Liver - Ascending Liver Yang
E217. Liver - Blood deficiency
E218. Liver - Blood stagnation
E219. Liver - Moisture heat in liver and gall bladder
E220. Liver - Fire
E221. Liver - Gall bladder Qi-Empty
E222. Liver - Cold in the liver meridian
E223. Liver - Qi stagnation
E224. Liver - Wind
E225. Liver - Wind with ascending liver Yang
E226. Liver - Wind with blood anemic
E227. Liver - Wind with extreme heat
E228. Lung - Qi deficiency
E229. Lung - Mucus-moisture in the lungs
E230. Lung - Mucus-heat in the lungs
E231. Lung - Mucus-cold in the lungs
E232. Lung - Dryness of the lungs
E233. Lung - Wind-heat attacks the lungs
E234. Lung - Wind-cold affects the lungs
E235. Lung - Yin deficiency
E236. Stomach - Bloodstagnation
E237. Stomach - Fire
E238. Stomach - Cold with liquid
E239. Stomach - Nutrition stagnation
E240. Stomach - Qi deficiency
E241. Stomach - Rebellious Qi
E242. Stomach - Yin Emptiness
E243. Spleen - Heat and moisture attack the spleen
E244. Spleen - Coldness and moisture affects the spleen
E245. Spleen - Qi deficiency
E246. Spleen - Qi deficiency + Declining spleen Qi
E247. Spleen - Qi deficiency + spleen does not control the blood
E248. Spleen - Yang deficiency
E249. Kidney - Heart and kidney no longer communicate
E250. Kidney - Jing deficiency
E251. Kidney - Kidneys cannot receive the Qi
E252. Kidney - Qi is not stable
E253. Kidney - Yang deficiency
E254. Kidney - Yin deficiency

For further information visit nutribook.info.

14 EBNS - Software for nutritional counseling

The main task of the database is to create personalized nutritional advice for each patient individually. The database was developed for Dietetics and Traditional Chinese Medicine.

The Database supports training and advices in the daily work routine.

The computer program provides lists of recipes, ingredients and herbs, which are given to the client. individually adjustable according to patient's request from whole food to vegetarians (lacto, ovo, ...). For every register there is an information sheet which can be given to the client. All texts can be individually designed.

The syndromes can be combined and result in an intersection of the recommended recipes and ingredients. The automated diagnosis for the TCM enables you to check your experience during the training as well as to confirm your diagnosis in the working day. You select several predefined symptoms and have the program automatically display the relevant syndromes.

How to work with the database:
Select the patient / client, select one or more of the syndromes you diagnosed and print the folder.

You can change all values, create new symptoms or syndromes, develop recipes, change or adapt ingredients and herbs to your findings. In simple client management, all relevant data about the person is stored. You get an overview of the past diagnoses and the development of the course of the disease.

As a consultant you save a lot of time when you print out the recipe, food and herbal lists for the recognized syndromes and give them to the clients. You can use this time for a personal conversation. With the database, dieticians and nutritionists can view the nutrients and trace elements for each recipe and develop recipes for syndromes even with suggested ingredients.

All recipe and grocery lists can also be ordered from me as a combination of several diseases. I wish all readers good luck, health and happiness in life.
More information can be found at www.ebns.at.
Volunteer: www.krebsinfo.at
Josef Miligui